To _____

From _____

....

....

....

Also for Kids…

A Book of Prayers for Kids: Ways to Talk to God Every Day (WordWay 2018), by Mel Lawrenz

50 prayers for everyday use. Prayers to start and end the day, mealtime prayers, and prayers for when we are ill, confused, lonely, or happy. Prayers for family, for friends, for school—and many other situations.

"My kids love this book!"

"I got this book for my friend's kids. It's just amazing."

WordWay
Knowing Him for Kids
Copyright © 2021 Mel Lawrenz
This title is available as a Kindle ebook.
Requests for information should be addressed to:
WordWay Resources P.O. Box 231, Waukesha, WI 53186

Published by WordWay Resources LLC
Cover and interior design: Sheila Hahn
Edited by Danae Templeton

Eva Helen Lawrenz (1987-2017) had a passion for truth, literature, and the world. "Eva" means life (Hebrew), and "Helen" means light (Greek). Life and Light Books are dedicated to her memory for the purpose of glorifying God through the ministry of the written word.
LEARN MORE: LifeAndLightBooks.org

Life And Light Books

CONTENTS

A WORD TO YOUNG READERS

Hello, friend! I am glad someone found this book for you.

There are certain special times during the year when we can stop and learn some very important things. Christmas is like that—a time when we think about how different the world is because Jesus was born in Bethlehem.

At Easter, we think about the end of Jesus' life. We think about the difficult things like how his enemies nailed him to a cross, and the wonderful things like his coming alive again.

What we learn at Christmas and at Easter is that Jesus is very different than any other person who ever lived. He was and is the Son of God. He healed people. He did miracles. And he offered us forgiveness and love. No matter who we are. No matter where we live. No matter how old we are.

This is a wonderful story.

This book is called *Knowing Him for Kids*. The best thing any of us can do is to keep on learning about what Jesus did and taught and how his enemies could not defeat him.

This book has 22 readings which you can do at any time, or you may do one reading each day starting three Sundays before Easter. If you try that and forget a day or two, don't give up! Just keep on reading. You can always go back and read the days you skipped.

The stories and ideas in this book are really big, sometimes a bit too big to understand. But that is okay. Just take in what you can. And maybe next year you will start all over. God bless you, friend!

Mel Lawrenz

A WORD FOR THE ADULT WHO GAVE THIS BOOK

It's great that you got this book for your kid, your grandkid, or your friend.

We often underestimate what children can take in. We perhaps don't even try to talk about the great truths surrounding the life, death, and resurrection of Jesus. But kids take in more than we imagine. If they are led to contemplate the life of Jesus every year around this time, the truths of the gospel will get planted deeper and deeper.

This book has 22 one-page short readings which can be done at any time, or can be a daily reading starting the third Sunday before Easter. If you and your kid(s) forget a day here and there, don't give up. Just keep with the schedule and come back to the missed days at any time. Next year you can do the whole cycle again.

Also, very importantly—the 22 readings in this book parallel the 22 readings in the original book, *Knowing Him*, which is for adults. If you talk to your kid(s) about the readings, you'll have more to go on if you read the adult version first. Blessings to you!

Mel Lawrenz

P.S. I am also enthused about another book for kids, *A Book of Prayers for Kids*. We are hearing stories from literally around the world of kids who are using the dozens of prayers in that book to deal with life and stay connected to God. More about it at www.WordWay.org

One day Jesus said: "I am the good shepherd; I know my sheep and my sheep know me—just as the Father knows me and I know the Father—and I lay down my life for the sheep." What he meant is that he knows us, he loves us so much, and he will protect us.

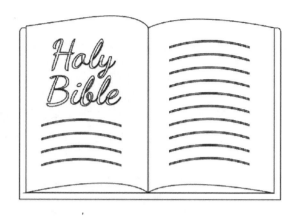

THE BIBLE SAYS...

It is for freedom that Christ has set us free.

Galatians 5:1

1
JESUS SETS US FREE!

Have you ever gotten stuck somewhere and could not get free? Maybe your foot got stuck in a hole in the ground, or you couldn't open a door that got stuck, or maybe someone sat on you and wouldn't let you get up. Now that is an awful feeling! But when you get free, it's wonderful!

Some people get stuck by fear that they have in their heart, or they have a hard time changing a bad habit. Maybe you have felt so, so bad for something you said or did to someone.

Here is good news! For everything we feel or think about that seems to have us stuck—Jesus came to set us free!

What does that mean? Read on day by day!

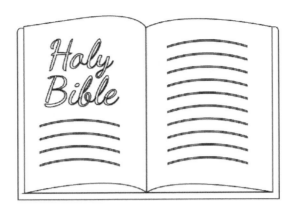

THE BIBLE SAYS...

"But what about you?" he asked. "Who do you say I am?"

Peter answered, "God's Messiah."

Jesus strictly warned them not to tell this to anyone. And he said, "The Son of Man must suffer many things and be rejected by the elders, the chief priests and the teachers of the law, and he must be killed and on the third day be raised to life."

Luke 9:20-22

2
GOD'S GREAT PLAN

Long, long before Jesus was ever born, God had promised his people that one day he would come to them to help them with all their problems. Someone would come to rescue them.

That day came when Jesus was born, so we celebrate at Christmas the coming of God's anointed one.

But that is not the end of the story.

Jesus told his disciples one day that he was going to be rejected and even arrested and killed. The disciples could not understand. Jesus just told them: This is what will happen. This is what must happen.

Sometimes it is hard for any of us to understand why difficult things happen.

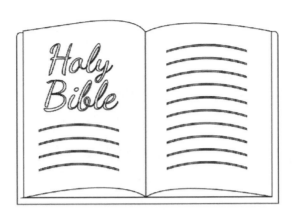

THE BIBLE SAYS...

"As the Father has loved me, so have I loved you. Now remain in my love. If you obey my commands, you will remain in my love, just as I have obeyed my Father's commands and remain in his love. I have told you this so that my joy may be in you and that your joy may be complete. My command is this: Love each other as I have loved you. Greater love has no one than this: to lay down one's life for one's friends."

John 15:9-13

3

HOW MUCH DOES GOD LOVE US?

Who can you think of right now who cares about you? Imagine someone who cares not a little, but a lot. They love you so much that they help you even when it is difficult for them.

Maybe you have heard a story of someone who bravely rescued a person who was in very terrible danger: a firefighter who goes into a burning building to save someone, a lifeguard who jumps in the water because someone is drowning, maybe a family member who donates a kidney.

Jesus told his disciples that there is no greater love than the person who will give his or her life for another. He told them that just before he was arrested and put on trial.

When Jesus entered the important city of Jerusalem on the last week of his life, he rode on the colt of a donkey. People cut palm branches and put them on the road. A huge crowd shouted "Hosanna to the Son of David!" Other people asked, "Who is this?"

When Jesus saw many people selling things in the area around the Temple, Jesus drove them away. The Temple was supposed to be a holy place for prayer and offerings. Not a place for a noisy, crowed market.

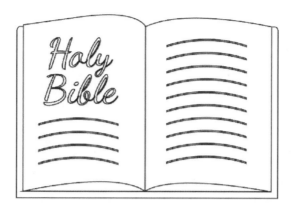

THE BIBLE SAYS...

Jesus entered the temple courts and drove out all who were buying and selling there. He overturned the tables of the money changers and the benches of those selling doves. "It is written," he said to them, "'My house will be called a house of prayer,' but you are making it a 'den of robbers.'"

Matthew 21:12-13

4
THE DAY JESUS WAS REALLY UPSET

Sometimes, when we see something that is really, really wrong, we get very upset—even angry.

That's what happened the day Jesus came into the beautiful courtyard of the Temple in Jerusalem and saw all kinds of people selling things there. It was noisy and stinky and embarrassing.

It is not wrong or greedy for people to have markets where they sell things, but those should not be in the holy Temple in Jerusalem! So Jesus chased them all out! He was the Son of God, and it was his job to correct people when they were really wrong.

Sometimes God has to clean things up. That is a good thing.

That was the way Jesus began the last week of his life in this world.

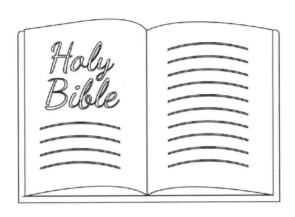

THE BIBLE SAYS...

The next day John saw Jesus coming toward him and said, "Look, the Lamb of God, who takes away the sin of the world! This is the one I meant when I said, 'A man who comes after me has surpassed me because he was before me.' I myself did not know him, but the reason I came baptizing with water was that he might be revealed to Israel."

John 1:29-31

5

JESUS, THE LAMB OF GOD

You have some relatives you know well, but maybe others you hardly ever see.

There was a man named John the Baptist who used to baptize people in the Jordan River. People came to him because they wanted forgiveness for their sins. Many, many people came.

One day, Jesus came to the river. John recognized Jesus, who happened to be one of his relatives. But he didn't say: "Hey, Jesus, good to see you!" John said: "Take a look, everyone! This man is the one who has come to take away our sin!"

The people had no idea what John was talking about. Years later they would, after Jesus died and rose from the dead.

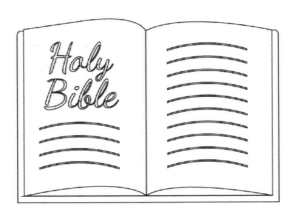

THE BIBLE SAYS...

James and John, the sons of Zebedee, came to him. "Teacher,"
they said, "we want you to do for us whatever we ask."
"What do you want me to do for you?" he asked.
They replied, "Let one of us sit at your right and the other at
your left in your glory."
When the ten heard about this, they became indignant with
James and John.

Matthew 1:20-21

6
HOW TO BE REALLY GREAT

Have you ever been around someone who was always trying to be first in a bad way? They cut in line all the time. They brag that they are someone's favorite. Maybe they want to be in charge a bit too much.

There was a terrible moment when two of Jesus' disciples, after Jesus told them that he was going to die and leave this world, said that they wanted to be above everyone else. What an awful time to be too pushy! The other disciples were pretty upset because James and John were just thinking of themselves.

Jesus told them all: If you want to be a great person, you have to give to other people and help them. That is exactly how Jesus treated other people.

No one needs a world with more pushy people!

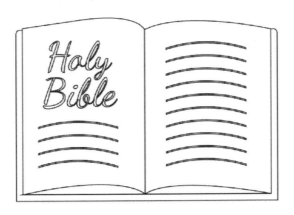

THE BIBLE SAYS...

"It was not with perishable things such as silver or gold that you were redeemed from the empty way of life handed down to you from your ancestors, but with the precious blood of Christ, a lamb without blemish or defect.... Through him you believe in God, who raised him from the dead and glorified him, and so your faith and hope are in God."

1 Peter 1:1819, 21

7

MONEY CANNOT BUY GOD'S LOVE

What if there was a time when you really needed to know that a family member or a friend loved you? Suppose you had this idea: What if I gather a bunch of money and give it to them? Maybe then they would love me. But how much is enough? Ten dollars? A thousand dollars? A million dollars?

Well, love does not work that way. The people who love others really well don't do it because someone pays them.

The Bible says that God is not looking for us to pay for him to love us. In some way that is hard for us to understand, Jesus sacrificed himself and showed us God's love. What we need to do is trust God about that. We need to believe not just today, but for our whole lives.

Jesus and his disciples gathered together in a
room to have the holiday meal, the Passover,
together. It was the last time Jesus could talk to his
disciples, and he taught them many important things.
He told them they should love each other always.

At that last supper Jesus washed the feet of his disciples. (We don't do that today, but back then people would take off their sandals and wash off their dusty feet.) It was Jesus' way of telling them that they needed to serve each other their whole lives.

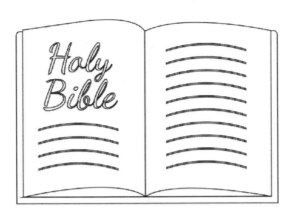

THE BIBLE SAYS...

"[Christ] is the beginning and the firstborn from among the dead, so that in everything he might have the supremacy. For God was pleased to have all his fullness dwell in him, and through him to reconcile to himself all things..."

Colossians 1:17-23

8

GOD SOLVES THE BIGGEST PROBLEMS

What do you do when you have a problem to solve, but you just don't feel strong enough to do it? Let's say the problem is getting along better with someone in your family, stopping yourself from saying the wrong thing, or getting your chores done sooner.

Sometimes it just does not seem to work to say: I'm just going to try harder next time. Sometimes we know that we need help.

The wonderful thing about Jesus coming into the world is that he helps us do things that we ought to do, but we just can't seem to do on our own.

One thing that we can't do on our own is forgiveness. We need God to forgive us. The good news is that this is exactly why Jesus came into our lives. He does for us what we can't do for ourselves. Wonderful!

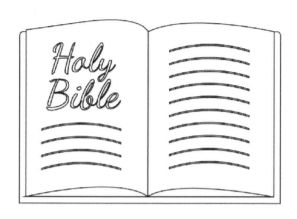

THE BIBLE SAYS...

Christ is the mediator of a new covenant, that those who are called may receive the promised eternal inheritance—now that he has died as a ransom to set them free from the sins committed under the first covenant.

Hebrews 9:15

9
OUR CONNECTION TO GOD

Have you ever had someone stand up for you? Has someone ever defended you or explained something that you did in order to prevent something bad from happening? We can all use friends like that!

The Bible says that Jesus does that for us. He stands up for us. You may remember from the Old Testament that there were many priests and that one of them, the High Priest, represented the people before God. (The word "priest" means someone who stands between us and God.)

Jesus is a new and better High Priest. He makes a connection between us and the God who created the whole world!

God wants us to be friends with him. Jesus is the link!

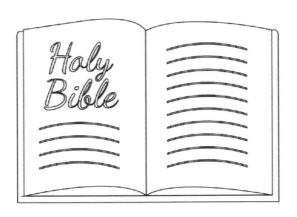

THE BIBLE SAYS...

Therefore, if anyone is in Christ, the new creation has come: The old has gone, the new is here! All this is from God, who reconciled us to himself through Christ and gave us the ministry of reconciliation: that God was reconciling the world to himself in Christ, not counting people's sins against them. And he has committed to us the message of reconciliation.

2 Corinthians 5:17-19

10
BECOMING FRIENDS AGAIN

It is wonderful to have friends but, once in a while, something bad happens and it messes up a friendship we used to enjoy. It could even be that someone said: I'm not your friend anymore.

Wow. That hurts!

And then you wonder. Is there anything I should do to fix this?

Believe it or not, that happens between people and God. People feel like they are so far away from God that they don't know what they believe.

Here is the BIG TRUTH. God created each and every one of us, and he does *not* walk away from us.

God wants to be friends! In Jesus, God has done what it takes to be friends. All we need to do is believe it!

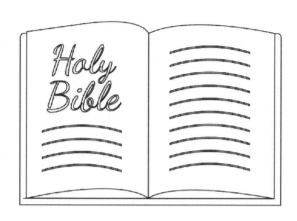

THE BIBLE SAYS...

"And I, when I am lifted up from the earth, will draw all people to myself." He said this to show the kind of death he was going to die."

John 12:32-33

11
JESUS TOLD US ABOUT HIS DEATH

Let's face it, it is really difficult to talk about the day when someone we love dies. Maybe you have had to face that with a grandparent, an aunt or uncle, or a parent—maybe even a friend. It is so, so difficult.

Let's try to imagine how difficult it would have been for Jesus' followers to hear him talking about his own death. He was a young man, after all.

But Jesus' disciples knew that there was a higher purpose to the likely death of their master and friend, Jesus.

Somehow we have to be sad about the death of Jesus, but also be glad that he told us how he would help the whole world through his death.

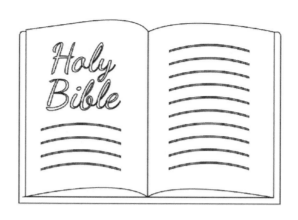

THE BIBLE SAYS...

Then Jesus said to them, "Why is it said that the Messiah is the son of David?"

Luke 20:41

12
A REALLY DIFFERENT KIND OF KING

The best king in the Bible was King David. He had many flaws, but he kept coming back to God. As a boy, he worked as a shepherd in Bethlehem, the town where Jesus was born hundreds of years later.

In Jesus' day, people were hoping that a new king would come very soon. A new king did come, Jesus, but he was a very different kind of king. He did not have an army or great wealth. But he was the true king sent by God, a better king than even the great King David.

Though we do not see him, Jesus is still king. He defeated all our greatest enemies—fear and sin and evil. And the best part is, we can count on his help any day of our lives.

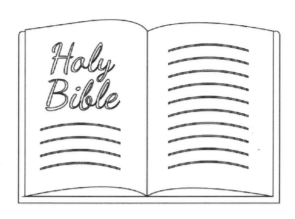

THE BIBLE SAYS...

Some of his disciples were remarking about how the temple was adorned with beautiful stones and with gifts dedicated to God. But Jesus said, "As for what you see here, the time will come when not one stone will be left on another; every one of them will be thrown down."

Luke 21:5-6

13

BEAUTIFUL BUILDINGS DO NOT LAST

In Jesus' day there was a huge and beautiful building in Jerusalem—the Temple. The white stones of the walls and the great pillars and the shiny metalwork made the building sparkle in the sun. This was where the people came to worship. There was only one Temple, and the people thought it would last forever.

But Jesus told them that one day it would be destroyed. (It was, about 40 years later, by a Roman army.)

There are things that do last, but not buildings. God will always be there for us. The love God gives us does not change. The promises of God will always come true. Jesus is alive with God the Father.

That is what we can count on!

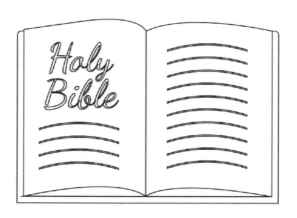

THE BIBLE SAYS...

May I never boast except in the cross of our Lord Jesus
Christ, through which the world has been crucified to me, and
I to the world.

Galatians 6:12

14
SHOULD WE EVER BRAG?

Maybe you know someone who likes to brag a lot. They are good at sports or get really good grades at school or have a very nice house. Those are not bad things, but it is bad when someone thinks they are better than you. No one should brag about how great they are, because God created us all and loves us all equally.

The Apostle Paul said that, before he believed in Jesus, he bragged a lot. He thought he was better than others because he followed all kinds of rules. But after he came to believe in Jesus, the only thing that he bragged about from that time on was how great and wonderful Jesus is.

Jesus gave his life for us. That is something worth talking to other people about!

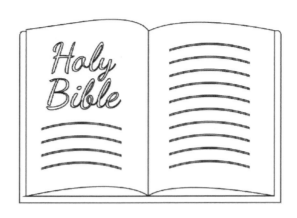

THE BIBLE SAYS...

All have sinned and fall short of the glory of God, and all are justified freely by his grace through the redemption that came by Christ Jesus.

Romans 3:23-24

15

MAKING THINGS RIGHT

There are lots of stories of people who break some laws and then are in big trouble. It is bad enough that they stole something or maybe hurt someone, but the real problem is that something is not right inside.

The Bible says that all people do wrong things because there is something not right inside. But Jesus came to make things right.

Jesus came so that we can talk to God and trust God and let God change us inside. Otherwise, there will always be something wrong inside. Through Jesus we are "justified," which means that things are made right between us and God.

This is right in every way! Let's thank Jesus for helping us deep inside.

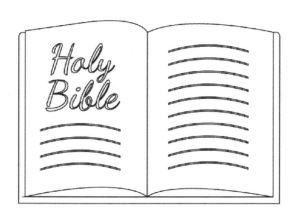

THE BIBLE SAYS...

We have seen his glory, the glory of the one and only Son, who came from the Father, full of grace and truth.

John 1:14

16
BACK TO THE BEGINNING

We are just about to think about the last week of Jesus' life on earth. But before we do that, let's remember where this amazing story began. Jesus' birth in Bethlehem was not just an ordinary birth. It was God coming to us in Jesus, a glorious Savior, someone "full of grace and truth."

A person "full of grace" is always kind, loving, merciful. A person "full of truth" never lies, is always honest, and tells you what you need to know.

Do you know someone who is like that? They are not perfect, but they love you and tell you the truth.

Jesus is all that, all the time. That's why we want to know him better and better.

Jesus knew his enemies were going to come for him and arrest him. He knew his mission was almost complete. So he spent hours in the night in a quiet place called Gethsemane praying to God the Father.

The enemies of Jesus put him on trial in the middle of the night. They lied about him because they wanted to get rid of him. It was all so, so wrong. They got Pontius Pilate, the Roman governor, to condemn him. But Jesus kept telling the truth.

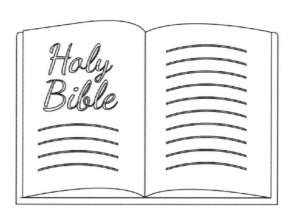

THE BIBLE SAYS...

"[Jesus] got up from the meal, took off his outer clothing, and wrapped a towel around his waist. After that, he poured water into a basin and began to wash his disciples' feet, drying them with the towel that was wrapped around him."

John 13:4-5

17
IT IS HARD TO SAY "GOODBYE"

Have you ever had to say a really hard "goodbye" to someone? Maybe it was a friend or a favorite teacher who moved to a different town. Or maybe you had a family member who died.

It really is hard, but we somehow have to go through it.

It was hard for Jesus' disciples to say "goodbye" to him. One day, they had an important meal together on the holiday called Passover. It was their last supper together.

Jesus told them many things that night. He also did a simple thing: he took a basin of water and a towel and washed their feet. Then he told them something very important: that they must serve each other, help each other, and care for each other.

They had to say "goodbye" to Jesus, but they still had each other.

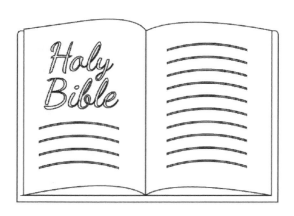

THE BIBLE SAYS...

"All this I have spoken while still with you. But the Advocate, the Holy Spirit, whom the Father will send in my name, will teach you all things and will remind you of everything I have said to you. Peace I leave with you; my peace I give you. I do not give to you as the world gives. Do not let your hearts be troubled and do not be afraid.

John 14:25-27

18
THINGS ARE GOING TO BE OKAY

That last evening Jesus spent with his disciples was a difficult time. They knew that they were going to be saying "goodbye" to Jesus because he was going away. They knew that it would be so, so hard.

But Jesus helped them. He told them that God the Holy Spirit was going to come among them, and that wonderful things would happen. He told them that they would have comfort and peace, not fear and distress. He told them that things were going to be okay.

The next time you have to face something really, really difficult, you can hear Jesus saying to you, "Things will be okay." You really can. Jesus the Son of God, God the Father, and the Holy Spirit make sure of it!

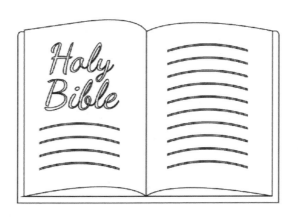

THE BIBLE SAYS...

A new command I give you: Love one another. As I have loved you, so you must love one another. By this everyone will know that you are my disciples, if you love one another.

John 13:34-35

19
WHAT IS MOST IMPORTANT

Sometimes we really need the people who help guide us and protect us to tell us what is most important. Sometimes parents or teachers will do that for us, but God gets the final word!

When Jesus met with his disciples in that room for the last meeting and meal they would have with each other, he told them *exactly* what was most important. He called it "a new command," and this is what it was: "Love one another."

Does that make sense to us? Can it be true that the most important thing that God wants us to do in life is as simple and clear as "love one another"?

Well, Jesus said it. We should trust him on this. It is pretty simple. God is love, and he wants us to love each other. That is what is most important!

The soldiers made Jesus carry his own cross. The Romans put to death many, many criminals in this way. But Jesus was not a criminal! He did nothing wrong.

Even while Jesus was nailed to a cross, he said some amazing things. He forgave the soldiers. He asked one of his disciples to take care of his mother. He said he was thirsty. He talked to God the Father. Finally, after a few hours, he died.

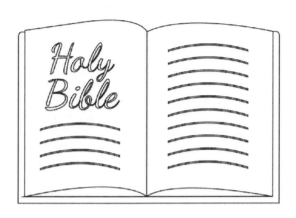

THE BIBLE SAYS...

When they had crucified him, they divided up his clothes by casting lots. And sitting down, they kept watch over him there. Above his head they placed the written charge against him: THIS IS JESUS, THE KING OF THE JEWS.

Matthew 27:35-37

20
HOW JESUS DIED

This is difficult to think about, difficult to imagine, difficult to accept. But here is the truth.

When Jesus was still a young man, people who were against his wonderful message about God coming to us were so opposed to him that they arrested him, put him on trial, and then killed him. Actually, they said terrible things about him, whipped him, and then used nails to fasten him to a wooden post with a crosspiece. They lifted him and put the post in a hole. A few hours later he was dead.

This was very bad, but it was the way the soldiers of the Roman empire put terrible criminals to death.

But Jesus was no criminal. He was King. He was the Good Shepherd. He was your friend and the one who forgives you.

And he still is today.

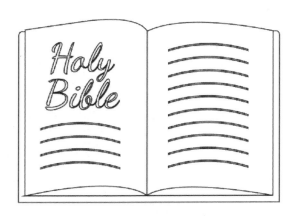

THE BIBLE SAYS...

At the place where Jesus was crucified, there was a garden, and in the garden a new tomb, in which no one had ever been laid. Because it was the Jewish day of Preparation and since the tomb was nearby, they laid Jesus there.

John 19:41-42

21
WAITING

Have you ever wondered what was going to come next after something terrible had happened? That is such a difficult time! It is hard to trust God then.

Just think about this: Jesus' disciples had followed him and lived with him for a few years. They came to believe that he was the Messiah, the man anointed by God to be new and better king and savior.

And then he was killed by being nailed to a wooden cross. They buried his body in a stone tomb above ground, with a huge stone rolled in front of it.

His followers waited. They did not know what would happen next.

They did not know, that on the third day, his tomb would be empty!

Jesus' suffering was over. His enemies went away, thinking their problem was solved. Jesus' friends scattered because they were afraid. But Jesus' story and his life was not over!

- KNOWING HIM FOR KIDS -

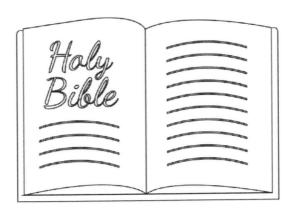

THE BIBLE SAYS...

Early on the first day of the week, while it was still dark, Mary Magdalene went to the tomb and saw that the stone had been removed from the entrance. So she came running to Simon Peter and the other disciple, the one Jesus loved, and said, "They have taken the Lord out of the tomb, and we don't know where they have put him!"

John 20:1-2

22
STILL ALIVE!

There were many enemies of Jesus who wanted to get rid of him and, even more importantly, to make everyone stop believing in everything he was teaching. Jesus had taught so many things that changed everything. He taught that what matters is what is in our hearts, not just what we do. He said that God loves every person, even those who other people reject. He hold us that God wants to be king in our lives instead of us thinking that human rulers can do whatever they want. And so much more!

Because Jesus came back to life on the third day after he was killed on the cross, we can know that God is mightier than anyone else and that Jesus is still alive. Every single truth he taught is still ringing like a clear bell all over the world!

All we have to do is listen and believe.

It was not difficult for Jesus to come back to life. The power of God is able to do anything. Some people thought the empty tomb meant that someone stole Jesus' body. But Jesus began to visit his disciples. They were shocked! Jesus taught them that he would always be with them, and that they could have peace in their lives.

Jesus left this world, going to heaven to be with God the Father. The last thing he told his disciples was that he was indeed King over all. He had all authority. He was stronger than his enemies. He told them to go and tell everyone in the world this wonderful news! That is what we need to do!

A PRAYER FOR EASTER TIME

Dear God, I believe in the Lord Jesus…

who was born in Bethlehem, who grew up and became a man, who taught crowds of people, who loved his disciples, who healed the sick, who was arrested by his enemies, was called a criminal, was nailed to a cross.

He died and was placed in a tomb; but on the third day, he rose.

I believe I am forgiven because of Jesus.

And I believe I can be strong because he is alive and is with me today. Amen.

From *A Book of Prayers for Kids: Ways to Talk to God Every Day* (WordWay 2018), by Mel Lawrenz

A PRAYER TO START ANY DAY

Thank you, Lord, for this brand-new day.

Keep me safe, keep my strong, I pray.

Guide my actions,

shape my thoughts,

tell me what to say.

Help me to follow your good, pure way. Amen.

A PRAYER TO END ANY DAY

Lord, the day is now over and I will soon go to sleep. You were with me through this day, as you will be tomorrow. Thank you for your blessings.

I'm sorry for mistakes I made. I rest in your forgiveness, and I ask for your help tomorrow. I pray for a good night's sleep. And I pray that tomorrow I can make a new beginning, walking with you wherever I go. Amen.

From *A Book of Prayers for Kids: Ways to Talk to God Every Day* (WordWay 2018), by Mel Lawrenz

A Book of Prayers for Kids: Ways to Talk to God Every Day, by Mel Lawrenz   available at Amazon.com

Dozens of prayers for kids to use for every day, difficult days, and special days.

Prayers include… A Mealtime Prayer – A Prayer to Start the Day – A Prayer to End the Day – Before You Read the Bible – When You are Sad – When You are Afraid – When You are Lonely – When You've Lost a Friend – When You Are Being Bullied – When You are Confused – When You Have Done Wrong – When You Accomplished Something Good – When Your Father is Not Doing Well – When Your Mother is Not Doing Well – When Someone You Love is Ill – On Your Birthday – To God Our Father – To Jesus the Son of God – To God the Holy Spirit – When Someone You Love Has Died – When Your Pet Is Ill – At Christmas Time – Thanks for Your Mother – Thanks for Your Father – Thanks For Your Family – Prayer for Faith – Prayer for Hope – Prayer for Love – Before Going to Church – When You Have to Say Sorry – About School – For the Beginning of the School Year – For the End of the School Year

- KNOWING HIM FOR KIDS -

- KNOWING HIM FOR KIDS -

Made in the USA
Columbia, SC
19 February 2021